Kick up Your Heels and Enjoy!

Retirement at Its Best

Beverly B. Thompson
Illustrated by James Cameron Dayton

GRANITE
PUBLISHING & DISTRIBUTION

Distributed by:
Granite Publishing and Distribution, L.L.C.
270 S. Mountainlands Drive Suite 7 • Orem, UT 84058
(801) 229-9023 • Toll Free (800) 574-5779
FAX (801) 229-1924

Illustrations by:
James Cameron Dayton

Production by: *SunRise Publishing, Orem, Utah*
ISBN: 1-57636-063-6
Library of Congress Catalog Card Number: 98-87459

Table of Contents

This book is dedicated to my husband, Jimmie, who supports me in my endeavors and doesn't mind being part of the story.

It is also dedicated to my children and grandchildren who continue to urge me to write and are my best critics.

A special thanks to my grandson, Cameron Dayton, to whom I am indebted for the clever illustrations and his loving support.

As we walk through the sands of time
we leave our footprints in the past,
and step forward into
a promising future.

Chapter One

Retirement Withdrawal

Breaking the habit of going to work every day is just like breaking any other habit. It carries with it a withdrawal syndrome. It isn't easy but it is doable. You don't have to wear medicated patches or go to a clinic. You simply have to face the obvious adjustments and make a bundle of decisions. Face up to the fact that any thing worth doing is worth doing well and you can make your retirement decision worth it. Enriching your life after retirement can be as rewarding as the pay raise, professional promotion, or perks were in your working career.

"So, who gets the blue chair?" was the question going around the building after my retirement date was set and my replacement announced. You have to understand that this chair had been my home away from home for several years. It was my security blanket. When the challenges of the job became great I could go to my office, close the door and sit in MY chair. It had been one of the perks of the job when I was appointed to be the principal of a large new elementary school. As I ordered furniture for the school I was allowed to furnish my office with furniture of my choice. The orange carpet already applied to the walls of the office left a lot to be desired so I had a friend paint a floral picture in pastel apricot and ordered a Navy blue leather desk chair and pull up chairs covered with a navy fabric. What else could be done with orange carpeted walls?

So it was that the blue chair had value to me. It had been my refuge and my favorite spot to regroup after a confrontation with an angry parent, an emergency with an injured child or a long vigil waiting for a bus to arrive to take students home. It was like a comfortable box I could crawl into to shut the world out for a brief period of time until the phone rang or the office door opened. It was also a symbol of my authority when an unruly child was sent to the office. They would be invited to sit in one of the pull up chairs in front of my desk as I sat in my chair making important decisions about the solution to the problems created by the perpetrator. That blue chair helped me experience (or so I thought) the wisdom of the ages in meting out fair judgements.

The orange carpet in other parts of the school may have had something to do with the unusual interest in the blue chair. None of the other members of the staff liked the color of the carpeted walls. No wonder they also wanted a nice blue chair to diffuse the orange brilliance.

Who wants to leave the work place in turmoil? In order to avoid chaos I immediately called my superior to make a simple request. “May I buy my blue chair?” I asked. Then I added in my most cajoling negotiating voice, “I am willing to pay the purchase price. I just have it nicely broken in to my body and I hate to leave it. As you may recall, it was your idea that I order it to my specifications when I was appointed to this position.”

After that most gracious offer you can imagine my shock to his reply. The firm, unwavering answer was, “No! It is against policy and procedure.”

Somewhere in the six-inch stack of policies I had read and almost committed to instant recall, there must have been buried some directive that precluded an administrator from buying the personalized chair designed for their comfort upon retirement. How could I have missed that? A Policy and Procedure book about the size of the IRS Tax Law Document must have had some small print that I deemed not worthy of my concern. Or I could have been distracted by some problem with a teacher or parent when I got to that part. It could have been on that day when just as I received a bomb threat, they brought two students in from the playground bleeding profusely and the pregnant teacher started in labor right there in the office. Well, obviously, my priorities were misplaced. I had missed the directive about not buying the chair but I still plead my case.

Buying the chair would be a win, win situation. I would have my comfortable chair, broken in to my particular needs (or body as it were). The purchasing agent would have money to buy my replacement a chair. It would fit my replacement's needs and that inevitable pecking order to claim the chair would be avoided. Apparently, they didn't care about win-win situations or saving money. After pointing out all of the advantages listed above my request was still denied. Of such are the hard realities of retirement. When you're gone, you're gone.

It is amazing how your strengths in negotiating deals diminish once you announce your retirement. Your brilliant ideas that have been received with enthusiasm suddenly become something to be taken under advisement. If they put it off they won't have to do anything about it after you're out of there. They can rework it a bit and present it as their own idea and get the credit. For years your presence at work each day has been a high priority to your employer, as if the place would close down without you. You have dragged yourself out of bed when you were really too sick to go to work because you were so vital to the operation. Now they are offering you some equivalent salary for unused sick leave and you can leave early. Wow! What a difference a day makes.

One of the first decisions that should be made when contemplating retirement is to decide what to leave in your workstation until the final moment of departure. It would be wise to clearly mark all of your personal possessions with your name and Social Security Number as well as the purchase slip taped to the back or bottom, as the case may be, to prove your ownership. You will likely be scrutinized by a thorough check of inventory or lack there of. You wouldn't want to spend your "Golden Years" in jail accused of taking things that belong to the company.

I wish I had bought my chair with my own money. With sales proof in hand I could have carried it out with my briefcase, the old coat and umbrella from my closet, the extra pair of sturdy shoes for supervising the playground, and that little sign on my desk that said, "BOSS." This is a lesson I learned in hindsight that you may benefit from as you approach "R" day: I'll bet you are already glad you bought this book.

The second item for consideration is the timing of the announcement. That depends on your personal taste. If you like to give people an opportunity to compose wonderful, sentimental goodbye speeches, invite family and friends to a retirement party and otherwise prove that you have accomplished something worth celebrating then go for the early announcement. That was my style and I still shed a tear or two as I read those cards and letters, look at the pictures and remember the wonderful people with whom I shared my professional career. In my case it was education and there is nothing like having a kid give you a hug and leave with a tear in their eye. It was even reported to me after a very touching going away party that a little child went home and told his mother I was going to die. When she asked him why he thought that he said, "they had a funeral for her today." Yes, I love tear-jerkers and never leave home without a hanky or a BIG box of tissues.

On the other hand, you may prefer to sneak out the back door, leaving your retirement decision on your desk for the custodian to find after work. They are always the first to know anyway. They are such good listeners when you need to pour your heart out to someone. Give him the opportunity to be the first to make the announcement for a change.

Then there is the testing of the water trick to see how much you will be missed. You've heard this one

before. Put your finger in the water and see how soon the hole fills when you pull it out. How disconcerting can it get? I personally hate that analogy. You spend a life time of your blood and tears making the world better and it isn't even noticed when you're gone. A good way to avoid this is to invite some of your friends from work to a post-retirement lunch. They are sure to tell you how much better things were when you were there. Well, in all honesty, it might have been. Who am I to question my good loyal friends? It's just as well that you believe them because it makes the memories of the next step a wee bit easier to take.

You walk out the door for the last time and you suddenly realize you have lost an important part of your identity. For years you have been identified by the kind of work you are paid to do. Now you have been stripped bare and that comfortable cloak of being someone who is known for a particular skill or position is no longer identified in that manner. Something about this reminds you of the fable about the Emperor's New Clothes. Was that coat of authority or identity a facade? Your question now is, "How much of me is the real me and how much of what I thought was me did I leave behind in my Navy Blue Chair?"

Let me tell you, it takes a while to get used to that moniker, "RETIREE" even if you have had communications from AARP since you turned fifty-five. Somehow, it seems that the real retirement day is a myth somewhere in a dreamed of future. Now it is really here and you have signed your name on the dotted line in the benefits office of the NEW Human Resources administrator. It might have been easier if your old friend in what used to be called "Personnel" was there to carefully ease you out the door with a hug and tell you she could hardly wait to join you in retirement.

Of course when those good loyal friends at lunch started talking about the last staff party and I was not a part of it I had to put a smile on my face to cover up the emptiness I felt inside. I felt like I had gone from "Who's Who" to "who's she?" But as soon as I was out of sight I took a deep breath and skipped to the car. I could have my own parties now and invite anyone I enjoyed being with. I wouldn't have to please the "fun" committee or the spouses of staff members who didn't want to be there anyway. I could see a bright light at the end of the tunnel of adjusting to retirement.

Few couples have the opportunity to retire at the same time. In our case my husband had a few years head start on me in the adjustment department. He had equipped the garage with all kinds of tools to make things. Not only did he stay busy in his workshop-garage but he also managed to have dinner ready for us when I got home from work. He was a good cook, but one of the things I had looked forward to upon retirement was spending time in my kitchen cooking. I had new small appliances that I hadn't even used yet. Well, let me tell you, it is not easy to reclaim your territory once you have given it up. He even had his own recipes stuck to the refrigerator door with a magnet that said, "His and Hers Kitchen."

Finally we came to an agreement; he would fix lunch and I would prepare dinner. That was fine with me because I bought a new sewing machine and computer just before I retired in order to make sure I would have plenty to do. I could take up my old love of sewing with the state of the art sewing machine. I also bought a new computer so I could write when my creative juices started to flow. If he fixed lunch I could work on my projects without stopping.

I had thought I could sew two days a week, write two days a week, have a day to play, a day to clean the house and a day for church. It sounded good and fit into the mode of the organizational pattern I had lived for the last thirty years, BUT I didn't take into account the part of retirement which is the most fun—FLEXIBILITY. I was to eventually get good use out of my new purchases but not in the orderly manner in which I had intended. I'm still trying to figure out how to do that fancy stitch on the sewing machine as well as the rolled hemmer that is designed to make an 8th inch hem. When I try it they turn out varying from 1/3" to 1/2" wide. Well I must admit that as I look back on it that simple straight stitch Singer sewing machine I made my wedding dress on was more user friendly. I wonder if I can find one in the good will store. You can imagine my disgust when I told my daughter and she said, "If you are serious we should look in the antique store." How's that for a put down? Get used to it. It is part of having lived history.

Not long after I retired we made the mistake of visiting a retirement community where all of the people were in wheelchairs and wearing oxygen tubes. The depression set in at once and my husband and I had to take a long walk and play a round of golf to make sure we were not on a banana peel skid. My heart went out to those dear people who needed the wheel chairs and the oxygen but my timing was poor. Somehow, I felt that the retirement decision had put me over the edge from being a vibrant, productive person to being ill and not able to care for myself. It comes to all of us eventually but statistics tell us that we are likely to live longer and have better health than any group preceding us. In fact, they tell us that the life expectancy for those born in 2002 will be eighty years. After ten years of busy retirement activity, I expect to live longer than that. I now realize that when we retire we just find other things to fill our time but we have more control over our choices. Most retired people wonder how they ever found time to work.

Some people insist that they will never retire. Self-employed people often make such a statement but if a son or daughter wants to take over the business, retirement seems more attractive. Many of our friends in this situation stay on as Chairman of the Board. They are a bit disenchanted, however, when they are not invited to the board meetings. Others find that the new generation sometimes takes more from the company than they, unlike you, are willing to put into it. That has been a disaster to some of our friends who had planned on using a part of the income from the company to finance their retirement.

A farmer I know, who is approaching ninety years of age, still wants to be actively involved in the farming decisions. His wife says he is finally willing to admit he is partially retired. On the other side of the coin we find people who have worked in situations where retirement is possible after twenty years so they are able to earn retirement benefits from more than one source. My heart goes out to those folks.

They have to experience retirement withdrawal more than once in their life. So what if they get all that retirement money to foolishly spend in their old age. Am I jealous?

Many newly retired couples plan to move from the big family home to something smaller. You may want to include visiting some retirement areas that cater to "Seniors" and are usually in a climate that lends itself to more pleasant living in the cold of winter or the extreme heat of summer. BEWARE; don't make a quick decision. Too many people, while still figuring out what retirement means to them, rush into a commitment with a heavy financial investment before they have tried it out. I would recommend that if you find a place that seems perfect, take time to check it out to see if it fits your lifestyle.

It is easy to make the big move into a retirement

area without thinking about hidden costs for amenities. You need to consider who your neighbors will be, if the life style of people there will be compatible to yours and if it is close enough to adequate health care, transportation, shopping and the type of recreation you enjoy. Most of these involve a much smaller living space, which may bring on chronic cases of cabin fever and cause you to hate your spouse after stumbling over him as you take turns moving from one room to another. Learning to share a bathroom after years of having your own facility can be quite disconcerting at times. My recommendation is that you rent or lease something for a few months for the winter season to see if it indeed fits all or most of the criteria above. We will consider this in greater depth in a later chapter.

Driving a recreational vehicle around the country may look like the best of all worlds and I have known some people who have done that for a few years after retirement, some successfully and others to disaster. The most dangerous thing you can do is to sell your house and invest all the equity into a recreation vehicle before you have tried "RV" living. All RVs need a live-in mechanic to keep the motor running as well as all the equipment included in these temporary homes working. They are usually not built to provide permanent, long-term living. The first criteria the manufacturer considers is constructing them as light as possible. That does not always mean sturdy or well insulated. Renting a RV for a trial run before you spend a chunk of your retirement money to buy one is the safest road to take.

If you can afford a RV and like to travel that way they are nice to have. You can see the country but it comes with a price. Driving in heavy, city traffic is a challenge as is driving in high winds and fast moving freeway traffic. Parking them on city streets or even in some parking lots is difficult. Campsites are sometimes hard to find and are often as costly as motels. Wives hate it because they still have to prepare meals, wash dishes and make beds without the conveniences of her state-of-the-art kitchen she left in the big house. She also has to do the laundry in the very public Laundromat. There you are, 'washing your dirty laundry' in public when you have been taught all your life not to do that.

Taxes are high on RVs. Gas mileage is usually about 10 miles per gallon making them expensive to drive. Traveling up steep highways or descending down a steep grade requires some special driving skills as well as adequate equipment. An under powered unit can bring you grief on the road. It seldom becomes a permanent way to live. In all fairness it is a way to see the country and if you can afford one and enjoy it, more power to you. (No pun intended.)

We purchased a twenty-four foot motor home

while we were still working. The selling pitch was that we could recoup our investment by renting it when we didn't want to use it. Now really, do you think I was actually going to let someone else take that cute little house on wheels when I wasn't along to protect it? Not on your life! As it turned out, after driving it around on the steep grades in the Rocky Mountains we didn't dare let anyone else drive it. We now know what it is like to be a snail on a race to the top of the hills. The air horns on large semi trucks are so loud and how is one to apologize to a truck driver for not moving over faster when you suddenly loose power on a steep hill. He didn't even smile back when I gave him that friendly wave as he finally pulled around us. I think the truck drivers call motor homes "Turtles." I'm not sure why, but I have learned not to stick my head out of the shell when a large truck passes us on a grade.

The first trip we took in our motor home after retiring was to the northwest and on to Vancouver Island for the salmon run. All went well until we started pulling up the steep grade out of the Columbia River basin. I guess when an engine anticipates trouble it gives off a warning signal which men call a backfire. What do I know? It just scared me, and as we limped up the beautifully graded highway a cloud of smoke seemed to be following us. My husband wisely pulled off the road on to what

appeared to be small gravel. A Highway Patrolman, bless his heart, pulled up behind us and told us to pull back on to the highway slowly. The bar pit gravel was known to have swallowed tires of large units making them hard to drive out. He said we were close to the summit of the hill and then it would be all down hill. He was so prophetic.

As we rolled down the hill and came to the first sign of civilization, a red light with a service station and convenience store, we felt safe and knew our troubles were over. Not so! After filling the engine with oil, getting some goodies to eat and pulling on to the road we realized the engine was coughing out the oil at a rapid rate. The small town ahead of us brought a sigh of relief. There on the main street of a small town, sporting at least four business establishments, was one touting car parts. After a cursory look at the engine, my husband closed the hood and walked quickly to the store without a glance back at me. He came back and said, "There's a mechanic around the corner." He always clams up when he is overly concerned about something. I admitted to myself at this point that we were in trouble and maybe he was wise to have been reluctant to take the trip in the first place.

Driving the sick motor home to the car doctor was pitiful. It limped and coughed all the way. Finally, we spotted a backdoor garage with several ailing cars parked indiscriminately around it. There was a lane that led into the garage and we pulled in, wondering what we would find. A dog came running out of the wide garage door, barking at this monstrous intruder. He flipped back as he hit the end of his chain. Little did we know that we

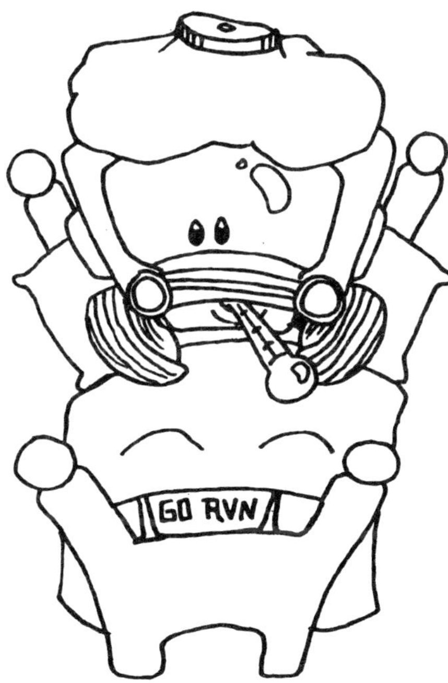

would spend the better part of a week parked in this spot. Its redeeming features were large trees providing shade, a long electric cord and water hose provided by the owner of the garage who was also a good mechanic. His hospitality was appreciated and he assured us we could live there in the motor home while he worked on it. He even brought us fresh salmon to cook for our supper. Where else would we live? There wasn't a motel in fifty miles and if there had been we had no wheels to get us there. We were stuck.

The next day he started diagnosing the problem. The covered motor is between the two front seats. Uncovering the motor and working on it required the front doors to be opened and our living space exposed to the workmen and any insects in the area. The first diagnoses was that some gasket needed to be replaced and it could easily be done that day. We should be on our way the following morning. Well it didn't quite work that way. I settled in for the duration, fixing meals, washing dishes, writing letters and sneaking into the bathroom when the men were taking their coffee break.

Several men in town enjoyed stopping over at the garage to visit, gossip and enjoy a coffee break together. They would lean in the cab of the motor home and look at the mechanic with his greasy arms up to his elbows in the caverns of the motor.

"What do ya think it is, Charley?" They would ask.

"Well, it wasn't the seal. Looks like it may be more serious. Maybe a piston." Charley answered.

The analysis of the problem became a neighborhood discussion. Finally, after major mechanical repairs we were on our way, but not until after, thinking it was repaired, Charley fired it up and black smoke filled the neighborhood. "Oh," he said. "I must have replaced the wrong piston." As I look back at the experience I laugh. We were the highlight of the quiet little town and there were times when I thought we might have to winter there.

The town was so small the post office closed for lunch and fresh bakery goods were delivered every other day to the convenience store. My regimen was to write a friend a letter, walk to the post office and every other day go to the convenience store to pick up doughnuts for the boys at the garage. One day I was laboriously writing in my journal and the men asked, "Are you writing a book?"

"No," I said, "But I may someday." They wanted to know if they would be in the book. Now they are.

Finally, we were on our way to Vancouver where we had more mechanical problems but did eventually meet our friends on the island at least ten days after the time we had agreed upon. The Salmon run lasted one day after our arrival and our friends left a couple of days later because they had to be back to work. We spent another week on the beautiful island, took the ferry back to the mainland and drove home. You can understand why we did not travel with a sense of security after our experience.

Well, we still have that motor home and even spent three winter months in it in a supposedly warm climate that the natives assured us had been very mild except for the winter we chose to spend there. With the cold wind whipping the sands around us and having to share the limited space for the better part of the day, we found that it was not fun. We even tried to enjoy it. I crocheted afghans and my husband watched a lot of TV, clicking from old westerns to the Stock Market report to ESPN for the sports scores. Just as I became interested in the old film and looked forward to the kissing end he flipped on to an update on the market and the ballgame scores. My unresolved feelings and complaints were simply answered with, "Oh, hadn't you seen that before? I knew how it ended." Finding some friends in the area saved our sanity and we learned from that experience that we wanted more than RV living in our retirement. I rest my case.

Sociologists publish lists of the events in the lifetime of a person that are associated with critical stress such as; having a new baby, a new work assignment, a death in the family, a life threatening illness, a move to a new city, or a divorce. At the top of the list for our age group is retirement. The grass always looks greener on the other side of the fence but in the case of retirement you may find that you have given up a comfort zone that was very rewarding to you in more ways than the financial security it provided. For some of us, knowing what we are going to do that day as we awake in the morning is the kind of security we enjoy. It takes a giant size leap of faith to retire. But it is worth it.

The fact of the matter is everyone that retires goes through an adjustment period. There are suddenly so many unknowns. Questions that plague us are numerous. Will my retirement check and Social Security allow enough cash flow for me to have a comfortable life style? Have I saved enough money in 401Ks, IRAs, stocks, etc. to take care of the big things that come along like a new car or some trip I might want to take? Is my Health Insurance adequate? What am I going to do with my time? *Can I stand to spend twenty-four hours a day with my spouse clicking channels?* Should I throw away my work wardrobe and buy new clothes? Or better yet! Will I ever be able to afford the kind of clothes I wore when I was working. Will my brain atrophy as I get older and don't use it as I have in the past? Can I play golf well enough to be invited to play with a group? How long do I have to live? Who will take care of me if I get sick? Should I move? Now I have more time to spend with my family, will they have time for me or enjoy having me around? That's why I decided to write this book. *It "ain't" all bad.* Life and enjoyment do not end when retirement begins. It is just the beginning of a new adventure and once you're over the shock of dropping into the ice cold water of retirement it can be quite invigorating.

Chapter Two
Making Choices In The Candy Store

I have real problems in a Candy Store. Since my favorite food bases are sugar and chocolate how can I choose between a yummy caramel covered with milk chocolate or a coconut bonbon? So it is with retirement. Have you ever had the experience of suddenly having a day all to yourself with nothing planned? The mental wheels start turning and frenzy overtakes you as you think of all the things you were going to do when you had a little time. A gripping mystery or romantic novel can appease you on such an occasion, but retirement is more than an unplanned day, it is the rest of your life. If you have religiously hung on to your Daily Planner then you can spend a couple of days making lists and prioritizing them as to what you should do first. I had a hard time giving up my planner but after constant teasing from my husband I settled for a modified version that I could keep in my purse and just sneak peaks at or jot down lists when he wasn't looking.

Most people start by making what I call, their guilt driven list first. Cleaning out closets and drawers are always high on the list. Organizing family pictures and balancing the check book, writing letters to people on your old Christmas List, redoing your address book, house cleaning INCLUDING washing the windows inside and out (heaven forbid) and taking all the furniture out of the bedroom for a good vacuuming. Which reminds me of a story I used as an "opener" years ago when I gave speeches to groups of women about making choices. You see, we are all quite alike in our avoidance choices. It seems that this little boy came down stairs, and looking at his mother with a very serious expression asked, "Didn't the Preacher in church Sunday say that from dust we came and to dust we will return?" "Yes," his mother replied. "Why do you ask?"

"Well, my ball rolled under your bed and when I crawled under to get it I found someone either coming or going."

In spite of our female urges to get everything clean and in order before we embark on a new adventure there are other choices you can make. Mine was to hire the girl who had helped me with my housecleaning when I was working. It would solve several problems if she came in and gave me a few good days of hard work. It was worth every penny. If she dusted over or around something and I didn't know it I would have no guilt feelings. Actually, she was very conscientious to the point of dusting the light globes and replacing those that were no longer working. I recommend this decision as you make your choices. You can't do everything yourself that you did thirty years ago. This goes for men also. Hire the neighbor boy to cut the lawn. I was now able to sit down in our nice clean house and make a list of what I thought I really wanted to do with the rest of my life.

I made an unbelievable list and yours may be similar to mine but I guess we each have our own dream list. Some of the things on my list were; travel around the world, make some memorable gift for each of my seventeen grandchildren, write a novel, write my mother's history, finish a quilt my mother and I pieced thirty years ago, find things to do to make my husband happy etc. Then I put the list aside and we went fishing to a mountain lake. Good fresh air would clear our heads and give us a new lease on life to start on our new road of making choices from all the possibilities that were out there waiting for us

With hands full of fishing gear, cold drinks and a portable chair for reclining by the water, we started down the steep bank of the lake. The water was lower than usual and some loose rocks made the descent a little precarious. It was *very precarious* for

me. I slipped and fell at a funny angle on my ankle. I was sure it was sprained. Jimmie helped me up to the campground where I rested in the motor home until he had fished for a while. He came back to the camp with his catch, I stood up to look at it and realized I could not stand up without excruciating pain. A trip to the nearest emergency room confirmed that the small bone in my leg had a spiral break and I needed to see an orthopedic surgeon. Two days later I was given my first retirement decision. I could retire to a wheel chair and cast for six weeks or undergo surgery. I chose the wheel chair.

We often find that our choices are modified by current events beyond our control. However, while confined to the wheel chair I was able to crochet afghans, read some books I had piled up to read someday, and let my husband enjoy the kitchen without my interference. He was so good to me, even taking me in my wheelchair to see my favorite football team play the big game of the season. It was during these weeks that I realized the most important thing I wanted to do in my retirement was to help my husband enjoy his. Happiness doesn't come by just satisfying our wants and ambitions but by giving of our selves.

Here again we find ourselves in a candy store of choices of what we can do to make life better for others. Opportunities are listed for volunteering in the local news papers everyday. Finding those that fit our talents and meet our personal goals takes some investment of time. Invitations to serve in various capacities will come to most retirees unsolicited. It is easy to say, "No, I am retired and want time to my self." That statement invariably comes back to haunt one as time goes on. Ten years after retirement I realize that some of those invitations that I choose to accept lasted only a year or two and I was on to something else. I had made new friends and made a contribution to the community.

I am reminded of a fine man who had spent his life in professional work. Upon retirement, he chose to spend the rest of his life promoting food banks for the needy. I had heard of his good work and reputation so when he called to see if my school would participate in the food drive I readily agreed. Every day I would encourage students to bring cans of food to school. Soon there were stacks of cans lining the halls so we found boxes and loaded them. I called this Good Samaritan and told him we had numerous cartons of food for the food bank. He said, "We'll be out to pick it up in the morning." To my amazement, he arrived in work clothes with a couple of young men. He took his turn and more carrying the boxes to the truck. He not only used his organizational skills to get the food bank up and going but also gave of his time and personal, physical effort to arrive at the goal. I tried to remember that experience when I was making my choice from the candy store of possible volunteer opportunities.

There are several good causes like the Heart Fund, Cancer Drive, Cystic Fibrosis Fund, Marathons for Children's Hospitals, Battered Women Centers, food or clothing projects for the homeless and programs sponsored by churches. Many of these are short-term commitments and/or contributions but still make allowances for a flexible schedule. Volunteering in schools, hospitals, libraries, church projects or docent programs for zoos or museums may require a longer time commitment. If it is something you enjoy doing, the length of the time involved is not a major factor.

Be careful not to be used by well meaning relatives who want to push their parenting responsibilities on to someone else. A week here and there to allow a get away together for some R and R or a business trip occasionally is justified. However, committing full time to tend grandchildren should be very carefully evaluated. It may be right for you or it may not. So many of our generation raised in the depression years are easily preyed upon for things to help others save money for new homes or to free them up from staying home and being parents. We learned from making sacrifices and we should give our children the same opportunity. Again, be cautious in your commitments.

All of us know that our retirement years may be somewhat limited and we have the right to fill them with some amount of freedom and flexibility. Grandchildren are some of our most precious people but they have the right to be raised by their own parents. That doesn't pre-empt our opportunity to spoil them with love and give our kids the benefit of our suggestions for good parenting skills. I am personally very good at giving advice, but by now you know that.

I have seventeen grandchildren and one year after retirement I made each of them a quillow on my newly purchased sewing machine. For those of you who have not run across a quillow, it is not a strange animal, but a small quilt that can be folded into a pillow. I carefully chose a fabric that seemed to fit the personality of each grandchild and made a quillow for his or her birthday. Some months I had to make four, other months less and a couple of months I didn't have to make any. Now many of the grandchildren are grown but I still find some of them using the quillows I made for them. That was the year that I was surprised with breast cancer but I had made a commitment to myself and I was able to complete it.

Give grandchildren recognition by covering your refrigerator with pictures and awards held in place by fancy magnets, visits for special occasions, a listening ear, a hug, telephone calls, birthday cards, holiday presents, and words of praise. Set an example for them by being a good person and someone they can be proud of.

One of the choices you may make is to share your retirement years tending a grandchild. If it is your choice it may bring you more joy than any other decision you make in life. If it is imposed upon you, you may resent it and that would be unfortunate for you and your grandchild. Remember, this book is about enjoying retirement.

Other choices and ramifications will be covered in other chapters of the book. Every day we make choices that are important to us and to those close to us. Be careful when you go in the candy store to make a selection of ways to use that precious time given to you after retirement. Make wise choices that consider your energy level, degree of health, your spouse's needs and your personal goals. Refer back to that list you made of things you would like to accomplish or do in your life. It will give you direction in your decisions.

You may not like all day suckers that use up too much of your time to devour and you may be allergic to the red licorice or just be sorry and feel guilty that you bought the liquor chocolates. On the other hand, a chewy caramel that you can really get your teeth into may be just the right choice. But they may be more than your dentures can manage. What ever your choices are enjoy them. My mother-in-law once told me that making your own clothes was a triple blessing of enjoyment. You enjoyed planning the item and buying the material, you enjoyed making it and when it was finished you enjoyed wearing it. So it can be with your choices in retirement. Read on.

Chapter Three
Garner Financial Resources

The love of money may be the root of all evil but it doesn't have to be. The wise use of money can make retirement years happy and productive. The old adage, "Save a little, spend a little and give a little away." is a good rule to follow. "Little" is the operative word. It is also relative to the size of what investors call, "Your portfolio." A decision to live on a poverty level or living high on credit cards are the extremes but the decision needs to be realistic in terms of your resources and expenses.

Money Management

Your money management pattern may not change after retirement but some people I am acquainted with became overly cautious about money upon retirement. They were afraid there would not be enough money to pay the monthly bills or taxes. Frugality becomes an obsession and with some affects their marital happiness. Others carelessly spend or invest the extra windfall they receive as they retire as if there is no tomorrow. There are many tomorrows and each one of them will be happier if wise money decisions are made.

Shortly after my retirement I was walking in a shopping mall with my daughter. We were following a couple I estimated to be in their seventies. They looked a little dowdy in outdated clothes. I turned to my daughter and referring to the couple in front of us said, “Don’t let me get careless and become dowdy. Make sure I wear nice clothes and make a good appearance.” My daughter started to laugh and said, “Mom, I know those people and they are very wealthy. They are also a fine, generous couple. I don’t think that it matters that they aren’t worried about wearing the latest style.” A wise daughter helped me see that people should not be judged by outer appearances. We can choose the retirement lifestyle that is right for us.

We all have the right to spend our resources according to our own priorities. However a problem can arise if you are not able to come to an agreement with a spouse about how to manage your money. Most couples in today’s retirement population have jointly contributed to the retirement nest egg. So in all fairness, decisions made about its management should be made together. You may not totally agree on whether to go for a hamburger and fries for lunch or to a pricey restaurant. Remember the negotiation skills you used while still working and use them now. You may take turns choosing your lunch or dinner venue. Senior rates are available at certain times of the day and the smaller size of entrees provides adequate food at an affordable price.

An elderly lady I heard about loves to go out to eat but she always takes a large handbag with her. She is known to have lined it with plastic bags so that she can fill them with the relishes, fruit, rolls and condiments at a salad bar. Then she zips the bags closed, chooses a few items which she pays for, sits down and eats an inexpensive lunch. Her dinner meal is in the handbag and she smugly walks out to her Cadillac and drives home. That is quite the extreme and even dishonest. I don't recommend it but it does illustrate the degree to which some retired folks go to save money.

The clothing budget that was a necessity while you were working can certainly be paired down but some new clothes can do great things for your mental health. You now have time to shop for the bargains and that can be a worthy goal in and of itself.

I have always hated to be tied down to a budget and the only way I could possible live with the constraints of a budget was to have certain amounts deducted from my paycheck each month for savings, house payment, taxes, etc. You may be more disciplined than I am and enjoy the constraints of a budget. Our money is deposited directly into our separate bank accounts and we each take responsibility for certain expenses. That is as close to a budget as we have ever been. I balance the checkbook each month and as we anticipate large expenditures we discuss how we will pay for them. It works for us but you may need things more tightly organized than that.

Having grown up during the depression, when there was never enough money to pay for the necessities, I have enjoyed the freedom of being able to splurge on an expensive piece of clothing or some

other foolish item. Occasional splurging and being irresponsible are two different things. Enjoy what you have but realize your limitations.

While you are working you always anticipate wages to rise, interest to rise on investments or valuation on real estate to go up. Having spent most of our working years in times of prosperity, but our childhood in the depression years and rationing and sacrifices during the war, we have experienced the extremes. What a diversity we have seen in our lifetime and hopefully we have learned enough to make wise decisions. It may take several months or a few years to find a good balance on which to make your financial decisions. By then you will know what your cash flow is and how your current investments are growing. Be careful not to put all of your eggs in one basket. Is that the advice you heard from your parents? It is still good advice and pass it on to your children and grandchildren. After all, by the time we have retired we have become so wise! Lets hope.

Perhaps it is advice I always remembered, having been raised on a chicken farm. If you filled the basket too full of eggs, they may crack, or, if by chance you dropped it, it was a disaster. When food and shelter money came from the eggs we gathered and sold we were taught to be very careful with them. So it is with our finances. Our biggest concern then was that an animal would get in the chicken coop and kill

the chickens or break and eat the eggs. Unfortunately, there are animals out there in the business world that would like to raid your financial coop and steal or misuse your nest egg. Be cautious.

Real Estate and Taxes

Taxes take a big lump out of the retirement budget even though some allowances are made for seniors. Property tax, sales tax and many hidden taxes take a large bite out of our income. Property taxes in many growing areas are very high. Reevaluation on the property where your home is located or other real estate holdings may rob you of money needed for living expenses. Look at it in terms of the benefits of holding on to it as an investment. If the real estate market is not progressive it may be the time to sell before your assets are depleted through high taxes. Above all, make sure you have a knowledgeable tax consultant to guard against you paying more income tax than necessary. You may choose to work out of your home on a part time schedule allowing you to realize tax advantages or there may be other tax advantages that your retirement status provides you. The tax laws change every year so your financial situation needs to be evaluated that often also.

Insurance Decisions

Look carefully at insurance policies. Many people are over insured or have money saved in insurance policies that pay very little or no interest and can be better invested in other ways. They may have been a very good decision when you were raising your family. With the possibility of your death when you had young dependants it was wise to have this coverage. But now those days are over and with the inflation factor, your money in insurance may be making big bucks for the insurance company but you may be getting a small piece of the pie. The value of the policy may not be available money while you are alive when you may need it.

Evaluate what health coverage you have. Some companies insure retirees but others do not. Some offer a continuation of health insurance at a price. Compare the price with other companies that provide supplementary health insurance. But make sure you have the additional health insurance that will cover your medical needs above what Medicare insurance will provide. It is easy to be talked into an excessive amount of health insurance out of fear of what the future will hold. There are foxes in the hen house of health insurance also. Get advice from more than one source.

I was asked to help with an elderly relative's affairs after she suffered a stroke and had to be cared for in a rest home. As I went over her affairs with another member of the family we discovered that she was paying for multiple health insurance policies. We also found that she had not applied for the insurance benefits from a deceased husband and son. She was paying for extended warranties on several appliances that were old and seldom used as well as insurance on a car that she could no longer drive. None of her health insurance policies covered her care in the rest home. Don't let fear drive your decisions on insurance.

Wise Investments

A good investment counselor is worth their fee. Be very cautious of the so-called investment counselor that has a deal too good to be true. IT IS! Most reliable brokerage companies have good counselors to help you with your financial goals. Don't be afraid to ask them what their fee is and what training they have had. You can get some evaluations and recommendations for your portfolio at no cost if they consider you as a potential investor. Make sure you maintain control of your money as long as you are able to make decisions.

Most of us have great concerns that we have a sizable estate to leave to our children. I agree with this noble thought but I also like that bumper sticker that says, "I'M SPENDING MY KIDS INHERITANCE." Our best investment in our children is to make sure they have an education allowing them to get employment that gives them a good salary and independence. There is something about children waiting around for their parents to die so they can live on "easy street" that is very disconcerting.

Family Trusts

The best thing you can do for your children is to have your attorney draw up a Family Trust. This is a document that you can change at any time you deem necessary. It insures that your wishes are taken care of in an equitable way that will not require long legal battles. Your attorney will also recommend that each of you make a will that identifies specific belongings you want each child to have upon your death. A living will should be taken care of also. This gives your family and health care provider directions as to your wishes in case you are not able to make a decision regarding life support procedures. Some hospitals are requiring living wills now upon admittance. It is a good idea to update these documents at least every few years. Something that your heirs will appreciate is an attached personalized letter that explains the monetary or sentimental value of each item and why you chose them to receive it. Some of these things can be gifts to them while you are still alive and you can tell them about the item. I have given my children some memory gifts as part of their Christmas for the last few years. It is delightful to go into their homes and see some of my treasures included in the decor.

CONTRIBUTIONS

The third side of the money adage is, "give something away." The ten percent rule is one many use. In my personal value system it is considered a tithe of my income, but regardless of your faith, etc. I can testify that the rewards or blessings received far exceed the contributions we make. There are so many worthwhile causes to which you can contribute money, and many choose to give much more than ten percent away. Some of the great philanthropists have provided libraries, museums, hospitals and schools which we have all enjoyed through the years. Most of us are not able to provide a gift of that magnitude but together with other donors, we can do great things to solve some of the problems of the world.

Do you remember the dimes we used to contribute to the Red Cross when we were in school? Even the savings bonds we bought during the war or the change we drop in the container for the Salvation Army is a reminder of the good that can be done when many people help a little. I am reminded of the widow's mite in the New Testament of the Bible which avows that the widow who threw in two mites which were equal to one farthing was greater than those who had contributed of their abundance because she had cast in all that she had. We may wish to give all that we have in energy, money or moral support but whatever we give, it should be with the spirit of a joyful heart. This is just another way to enjoy your retirement years.

Chapter Four
The Travel Agent —Your Friend

Lighten up. Retirement is fun and new experiences are around every comer if you open your psyche to a new approach to living. The best way to do that is to get well acquainted with a travel agent. Preferably one like ours that travels with you to new locations, one who likes being with people and having new experiences. Honestly, it is fun to travel with a new group of people to new places. You learn something about how you fit into a group, the kind of people you enjoy and those that you find have interests in common to your own.

Many tours are built around specific interests. Some are to historical areas like Washington D.C., Valley Forge, and/or Philadelphia. Several are available to a special entertainment location such as Branson Missouri or New York City. Experiencing fall in the brilliant colors of the Northeast or a train trip across Canada may be of interest to you. If you haven't seen the dynamic varieties of the canyons and parks in Colorado and Utah you haven't lived. Pictures can't even begin to fully represent the beauty and feeling you experience by being there.

There are trips available to any place in the world. Some even to outer space and that is where my husband would like to send me sometimes but I've already told him I'm not going alone. I did go on a tour without my husband to Egypt and Israel but my daughter and son-in-law were on the tour. They were great but I did miss my husband and wished he were there so I would have someone to hold on to if I rode a camel, which I didn't because I didn't have anyone to hold on to. I did need someone to hold on to as we visited several other places on the tour.

I was almost abandoned in the ruins of the old city of Memphis. After looking at what was left of the monuments to the Egyptian rulers my fellow travelers and I walked over to the little tourist tents. Tourist trappers who wanted to sell me trinkets immediately surrounded me. The brief purchase I made seemed to take only minutes but as I looked up, the bus was pulling out. You can imagine the terror I felt, being on the other side of the world among a few money hungry tourist vultures that just wanted my money and I couldn't even speak their language. Luckily, my daughter noticed I wasn't on the bus and convinced the driver to stop and wait for me. Boy, did I sprint for that bus after pushing my way out of the entrapping circle. Gasping for air, I trudged back to my assigned seat behind my daughter and son-in-law. He said, "Oh, I'm sorry, I thought you were on the bus." Apparently he was the one on the bus assigned to count heads. His count should have been one short because *I wasn't there*. He is a bright man involved in research projects requiring specificity in dealing with numbers. Was this a ruse to lose his mother-in-law? One will never know. I'll tell you, I was the first one on the bus after that.

As it turned out that trip is one of the most interesting things I have ever done and I am happy that I decided to go. I am still sorry my husband wasn't with me. We have been on several trips together since. He is a good roommate even if he does snore. Somehow his snoring doesn't bother me nearly as much as the snoring of the lady that shared my room on the Israel tour. How was I to know that no one else would room with her because of her snoring? She confessed that to me right up front but I was sure it wouldn't bother me after living with it for almost fifty years. Snoring and sawing down a whole forest of trees every night are two different things. Also, I was a little shy about getting out of my bed, walking across the room and punching her in the ribs with my elbow. I did think of the pillow-smothering trick several times. Tip to the traveler; check out the person you agree to share a room with before you make a commitment to spend ten nights listening to them inhale with a gasp, hold their breath, exhale with a rumble like a railroad train over bad rails and then the loud snort. Why do I remember those details?

I read the lists of possible trips my travel agent friend gives to me like the menu at a restaurant. I am interested in cruises on the oceans to Alaska, Panama Canal, Hawaii, Bahamas, Mediterranean, and other far away places. Flights to Europe, the Far East, South America, Australia or even to far off Mongolia where some friends told us of the unique experiences they had in that remote place. If you have a taste for a truly rare cuisine, visit the Gobi desert and have the nomads there prepare dinner cooked in a sheep's bladder. It is only a hundred miles or so from the heavily populated area of Mongolia. Transportation options are open. One may be a camel train. How about that trip for fun? We are retired and the world is ours to see and enjoy as far as our newfound freedom and finances may take us.

We enjoy trips to Branson, as do many retired people. Sitting in those large congregations of retired folks is, as the kids say, "Awesome." Thousands of listeners enjoying good, clean entertainment that pleases the auditory senses without blasting them out of their seats or causing them to blush with embarrassment. Someone has said, "The government could solve the problem of Social Security and Medicare by dropping a bomb on Branson." As we look over that group, however, we realize they are the people who's hard earned money had built the coffers of the Social Security and now it is their turn (our turn) to enjoy the fruits of their contributions. I have learned to appreciate those entertainers; restaurateurs, travel agents, health providers and others who help provide for the good life of we retired people. Yes, it is good business for them but I for one am glad that they chose to invest their money and efforts into our needs.

Extended families are now scattered far and wide across the world. In the olden days, (our olden days) families used to live by each other for a lifetime. The family farm or business would be divided up between children and grandchildren. Some towns had very few people in them that were not related to each other in some manner. We now send our children to the college of their choice, they meet someone from a far away city, get work in a far away state or country and even have our grandchildren when we don't live next door. We'll deal with that in another chapter but for now it has a lot to do with traveling.

The average couple with the average family of four children can now have four different places to visit once or twice a year. At one point we had one in Pennsylvania, one in Florida, one in California and the other in Utah. Transfers have taken them to Iowa, North Carolina, Georgia, and Michigan. There are few states we have not been to or through as we have traveled to see our children and grandchildren. A fast car trip across the states to be somewhere for a special occasion on a few days off from work, allows you to see a lot of yellow lines on the freeway, billboards, road signs and traffic. Someone said the Interstate Highway system allows us to cross the country without seeing anything. Quick weekend flights make you knowledgeable about the way to get around airports to meet connecting flights and the fastest way to get from the airport to the neighborhood where your children have found a home. A hug and kiss from the kids and grandkids makes the trip worth anything you paid to get there. Seldom do you have time however, to see or do the things you can do on a tour.

Traveling with people who can lead you through the maze of ticket lines, find the best restaurants, a nice clean motel and the most scenic way to get from one attraction to another makes the trip enjoyable. You don't have to drive the car or navigate for the driver. Nor does anyone get angry with you because you told him to turn at the wrong place and now you can't get back to where you were to find the right turn. Nor do you have to stop at service stations to ask directions after driving around for thirty minutes or more. Your tour will be more fun if you have been a designated navigator in the past to take a map with you to see where you are and how far it is to the next destination. If the travel agent doesn't provide a map for you there are plenty of tourist traps that will sell you one for twice as much as they cost in the discount store back home.

Spending a few hours at a time on a tourist bus can be fun and restful. Many of them are equipped with TV screens and they show movies or videos of the places you are going to visit. A good book to read is a wise purchase. Some groups have sing-a-longs and almost all of them provide some time for people to introduce themselves and tell jokes or stories. You can always take earplugs if any of those become an annoyance to you. There is a restroom in every bus for emergencies but they make frequent rest stops. Most people like to get out and walk around at least. Some take a small cooler chest with them to have a drink handy or carry medicine if it has to be kept cool. Every tour we have been on has had someone in the group who has some medical skills. Bus drivers have CB radios and some carry cell phones to call for emergency help if needed.

Long bus tours involving a week or more with full days of traveling requires the strength of the strong and the brave. If you are not a good traveler and/or have trouble with swelling ankles or sleeping in a different bed every night you may opt not to take the long bus tour. Instead you may choose the tour that flies you to the closest city to your destination and just uses buses to shuttle you from the airport to the venue.

Some of the advantages of tours are the way the luggage is cared for, scheduled departure times and special food if it is needed. Most of them have luggage pickup and delivery to your motel or hotel room and all gratuities are paid as a part of the price of the tour. You will also receive a list of how many meals and nights of lodging are included. Arrangements can be made for those requiring special meals. We have traveled with many diabetics and they have been considered in ordering food.

There are time constraints and it is important to be ready for bus departures. If you like to stay in bed late in the morning you may have to skip breakfast or have a roll and some juice in your room. Wake-up calls are usually arranged for by the tour guide so that everyone is called in plenty of time to be ready for the day, eat breakfast and leave at the scheduled time. Many accommodations provide a continental breakfast that you can pick up and eat on the way to the bus if necessary. It is possible to be the object of unmerciful teasing if you are always the last one on the bus. Take it from me. I have had experience.

One cost that is not included in the price of the tour is a tip for the bus driver and tour guide. A contribution of two dollars per day for both the driver and the tour guide is the going rate. Someone on the tour usually initiates the collection on the last day of the trip so don't spend all your money in the tourist shops. I have had experience here also. It is quite embarrassing to ask the tip collector if he will accept your credit card. But then again, you may never see him again in your life. Some of us are very good at living with the memory of embarrassing episodes. I only share these to help you avoid my penchant for goofs. There is one in every crowd but my husband really wishes I wasn't the "one".

My travel agent friend tells me there are several ways to save money. Airlines offer frequent flyer points and many of them give senior citizen discounts which some of them call senior discount coupons. On occasion they offer one-day discount specials and similar specials during the off season. Travel agents seem to know about these before the general public so it pays to plan ahead and let your agent know what to watch for. Your travel agent may provide you a way to earn a free tour fare or a discount. Special fares come as code share fares, super savers, hidden city tickets, senior citizen discounts, companion fares, comparison fares, discount coupons, and alternate city tickets as well as others that may be offered in the competitive world of air fares. Calling airlines directly gives you only the options that airline is offering whereas a travel agent can compare all the options.

Several retired folks we know plan on at least one special trip a year and budget that into their financial plans. One little old lady I know of takes several a year. She informs people on the tour that her husband never took her anywhere but left her a bundle of money and she is spending it all on seeing the world. Now, in her late eighties, she pays for a companion to travel with her and the last I heard had at least two lined up for the next month. She no longer drives but starts and revs up the motor of the big sedan in her driveway every day she is home. She never was allowed to drive it and seldom rode in it. Now she

gets a big charge out of starting it up and sitting in the driver's seat, gloating. Is it for sale? No way!!

Travel agents are always good for an unbelievable story and I can hardly wait until we have lunch again to hear another one. I'm going to invite my husband so he can hear about all of the advantages of going to Mongolia.

Chapter Five
Taking Care of Yourself

Kory was a new student in the school. He had moved in from another part of town where the kids were a little tougher and had to fight their way to success. He had a difficult time adjusting to trusting friends and teachers. This was a strong family oriented community that for the most part, taught their children respect and a value for education. Kory brought with him some negative attitudes and nonconformist behavior that landed him in my office on several occasions. My style was to work with him in a positive, problem-solving mode showing him how to make friends and cooperate with teachers. The punishment he expected and did not receive threw him off guard and before he knew it we were friends and he was more compliant. His visits were less frequent but I saw him almost every day and always spoke to him. He was one of my success stories.

One day, as I walked down the hall, he ran out of his class and put his arm around my waist. "Somebody just told me you were going to retire."

He said as he looked up at me with a puzzled expression.

"Yes," I said. "This will be my last year as principal in the school."

"But, but you are not old enough to retire." He stammered.

I assured him I was eligible for retirement but I would miss being with the students in the school.

He stood away from me then, looked me over and said in his authoritative voice of experience, "You sure have taken good care of yourself."

"Thank you," I said, trying to hold a straight face. "You had better get back to class now."

I left him walking back to his class and hurried to the sanctuary of my office to compose myself. I looked in the full-length mirror of my closet door and decided this had to be one of my better days. Perhaps his evaluation wasn't too far off. Then I shared the story with the girls in the office. They didn't dare laugh out loud but they were very amused.

I am afraid if I saw Kory now, after ten years of retirement, his evaluation would be altered. Of course, he has had ten more years of experience also. I include this story because I have often thought of that comment and wondered what I needed to do to take good care of myself.

Gravity does a number on all of us and there isn't a lot we can do about that. I did have an estimate from a plastic surgeon about a whole body redo but the price was way too much to pay since my insurance wouldn't chip in a dime. Those insurance evaluators are something else, aren't they? I tried to convince them it would save money in the long run. They wouldn't have to pay for counseling which resulted from deep depression, but they wouldn't buy that or pay for it either. I found the best solution was to hang out (excuse the expression) with people my own age and approximate size and shape. I move in a very limited circle.

It is important to have a thorough physical examination when you retire. We often put things off when we are working and one of them seems to be preventive health care. A yearly checkup is important as we age and more often if your health care provider or you feel it is necessary.

Both my husband and I have avoided fatal health problems because of early detection and good medical care. Our last visit however was most disconcerting. He had lost two pounds and I had gained two pounds.

There is no justice in this life but I guess the scales don't lie. I do wish they would use the kind I have in my bathroom that I can adjust by leaning a little to one side or the other. And then, I always forget and wear heavy clothes to the doctor's office. Since all of the other things they found out about me from that blood sample was OK I have nothing to complain about.

Taking care of ourselves involves more than just health. We have to take care of the little things that bring joy and self worth to our lives. As I told my podiatrist the other day, "I can be happy if I can get my hair done every week, my fingernails done every other week and have him take care of my feet every few months." That is not too much to expect out of life. The counseling you can receive from a car-giver on a regular basis can help you avoid that deep depression syndrome to which I referred earlier. Have you ever known anyone wiser than a beautician or a barber? They are such good listeners.

In all seriousness a good podiatrist is important to us as we age. Many serious foot ailments can be avoided by regular care. We all know that walking is probably the very best aerobic exercise and that requires healthy feet and good walking shoes. When our bodies become less flexible it is more difficult to personally give our feet the attention they need. Some of us, not mentioning any names, can't touch our toes the way we used to let alone look at the bottom of our feet. It is extremely important for those suffering with diabetes to take care of their feet. They sometimes loose feeling in their extremities and abrasions do not heal easily. A small thing like a toenail clipped into the quick can cause problems.

When you have questions about your health, write them down so you don't forget to ask the doctor about them when you see him or her. Changes in normal body functions can be important and should be noted. He or she doesn't see you often and may not notice subtle changes that are apparent to you.

Take any medicine as it is prescribed. Finish the regimen schedule for the antibiotic's prescription. Your body can build up an immunity to the medication so it may not be effective another time. If you have been on blood pressure or heart medication for a period of time do not stop taking it without consulting your doctor.

Our common health problems seem to be the favorite topic of discussion as we get older and it is an important concern but we can let it overwhelm us if we are not careful. Some of us may be accused of enjoying poor health because that is all we talk about. As they say, "Get a life." If you find yourself in this category, try to think of ways to change the subject and discuss something more delightful. I have a friend that always has a good joke on hand about any ailment and I find that much more therapeutic than a sad, cajoling expression of understanding. I wish I could remember those jokes. I can't, but I can remember laughing. Need I remind you again that this book is about enjoying retirement?

Sometime I think I will tape-record a session of friends talking about their operations. I have to admit I have been known to play, "Can You Top This?" in the operation comparison game. I can hold my own with at least seven heart-rending experiences. If I need a 'ringer' I can always throw in a few of my husband's. One thing I am sure of is that the next time they start rolling me down the hall on a gurney to the operating room I will be kicking and screaming about how I was never going to do this again. Those shots are so calming though and they always put me to sleep before I see what's coming.

No one seems to get out of this life easy and I for one am thankful that we have such good medical care to make life as pleasant as it is for us.

Now to the subject of diet and exercise: I think I will skip this one because we have all heard it before. We have taught our children and grandchildren to count by counting the necessary food groups in our diet. And now I pick up the paper and they inform me that older people loose their taste for most everything but sweets. I knew that from experience but I didn't want to admit it. In fact I was mulling that over in my mind last night when I couldn't sleep and got up to eat two cookies. It was very disconcerting to take away my guilt feelings for choosing to eat sweets by telling me it is just because I am getting old. I like chocolate too! Somewhere I read that chocolate is soothing and will help you sleep. I wonder where I hid that box of chocolates.

Hearing loss seams to come to most of us as we age. We miss so much in life if we can't hear the sounds around us. Research tells us that women speak twice as many words a day as men. When I told that to my husband he said, "What?" Obviously, we speak twice as many words as men because we have to repeat everything. I'll tell you, we have had some good laughs about being misheard. It can also cause problems and misunderstandings. Hearing tests are painless and they are worth the time and money to have one. I wouldn't begin to tell you all the possibilities of hearing aids. There are so many on the market and some of them are very expensive. I do recommend that you have an evaluation by a qualified ear, nose and throat specialist.

A funny thing happened to us one day. We were shopping for a black hat for my husband. Not finding one he liked I said, "Maybe you would like a black hat for your birthday."

His response was, "What do I want with a back pack?"

An audiologist would probably diagnose his hearing loss. I didn't have a clue but we sure had a good laugh over it.

Being able to enjoy our retirement years involves a lot of hearing and seeing. Which brings us to the subject of vision care. Our eyes are so precious and the vehicle to so much happiness in our lives. Modern medicine can do so much for eye care. Cataracts seem to creep up on us and the correction is much simpler than it was years ago. Glaucoma tests are also recommended on a regular basis. Even though our vision does not usually have dramatic changes we should have an eye evaluation once a year.

New talking machines are just coming on the market that read the small print for us on medicine labels, scales (who wants to hear that?), clocks, etc. Now if they would just invent child proof medicine bottles that can be opened with arthritic hands and shrink-wrap that will yield to dentures we can really be happy.

Living with the changes in our bodies and keeping a good sense of humor about it will help us keep it in perspective. Joking about it doesn't make it go away or replace the need for attention but it does help us to cope in a healthy way. All these health needs that thrust themselves upon us require that we live in an area with good medical facilities. Which brings us to the next chapter which is deciding where to live after we retire.

Chapter Six
Where Do You Want To Be When?

One of the questions we face after retirement is do we stay in the large family home where we have raised our families, enjoyed extended family parties for holidays, entertained our circle of friends and enjoyed decorating and even remodeling? It has been the center of our universe for twenty or thirty years and part of our personal identity. Our addresses and our telephone numbers identify us.

Things to Consider When Selling the BIG House and Moving

My first suggestion is that you not make the decision the first year or two after retirement. You might consider the following questions as you evaluate the wisdom of a move.

1. Can you handle the emotional stress of leaving your home?

2. Do your family members live close enough to continue to help you enjoy your home?
3. Are your friends still living in the area?
4. Is your health and energy level such that you still enjoy the yard work and house work?
5. Can you afford to hire the yard and housework done if you are unable to do it yourself?
6. Is your house increasing in real estate value?
7. Have property taxes increased faster than the value of the house?
8. Will the responsibility of owning the home limit the flexibility you want in your retirement years?
9. Can you leave for months at a time and be assured your house will be safe from vandalism or theft?
10. How much of your retirement cash flow does it take to remain living in this home? Consider taxes, utility bills, homeowners insurance and maintenance. If the house is not paid for add the payments to your list.
11. How does the location of the house fit in to the local development plans for the future?
12. Is the weather a factor in staying in this location?
13. Are health facilities, shopping, recreation, public transportation and the church of your choice close enough for you if you can not drive a car.

14. Could you live in your house if you were confined to a wheelchair or had to use a walker or crutches?
15. How often do your family members, friends or neighbors stop by?
16. Do you and/or your spouse enjoy being in your home alone?
17. Do you feel safe in your neighborhood?
18. Do you know anyone who lives close to you that would help you in an emergency?
19. Do you experience annoyances in your neighborhood that would be a factor in moving?
20. Are you involved in community activities that you are not willing to give up?

There may be other questions or considerations that are important to you that may surface as you consider these twenty questions. As individuals you all have your own value system. No one else can make the decision for you.

In Chapter One I told you about my experience with a broken leg shortly after my retirement. Our home had a front split-level entrance with two complete finished floors up eight stairs and down eight stairs. If we entered from the garage at the back of the house we had to go down four steps and up two stairs. You can imagine the challenges that created for me confined to a wheelchair and for my husband to help me. We were fortunate that there were bathrooms on both levels and the master bedroom was on the top level, which also included the kitchen, living room and study. It was also most accessible to the garage entry. The laundry and big screen TV were down stairs along with guestrooms and another bathroom.

A portable telephone made it easy to answer the phone but if I was alone in the house and the front door bell rang I would usually have to ignore it. If I found it was really necessary to answer the door, which we kept locked for safety, I would have to lower myself from the chair to the floor and slide down one step at a time on the seat of my pants. I would use my good foot and hold on to the banister for leverage. (Cameras were not allowed in the house during this period.)

I was fortunate to have a husband who could do the laundry and cooking and was willing to do them with a smile. We had a lot of laughs about awkward moments in the bathroom and I was often reminded that there are times when my independence was tied to my ability to stand on my own two feet. It was a six week endurance test but opened our eyes to the problems we may face if we chose to spend the rest of our lives in that house.

It was a house in an area surrounding a beautiful golf course and at the foot of the magnificent Wasatch Mountains. Our large windows provided us a view of the towering peaks covered with pines, oak brush and aspen. Every season was one of beauty from the fresh spring greens to the brilliant fall colors and the snow covered mountains of winter.

On the other hand, the house was on a sloping, corner lot where snow was piled high by the snow plows, sidewalks on two sides of the lot had to be cleared of snow and during lawn mowing season it meant pushing up hill at least half of the time. Tax assessments were based on property evaluations that exceeded the market value of the house. It was a great house for a young family but it had definite problems when considering it for a retirement home.

We decided to try some alternatives but we took about five years to make a permanent change. We lived six months, April to October in our northern home and six months in our winter or southern home. Many of our friends were doing this but eventually we found it to be an unnecessary burden to maintain two houses. We gradually weaned our selves away from the ties that kept us in the big family home, finding more reasons to stay in the smaller retirement home. The experience we had in making this decision helped form the following questions. They are similar to the list above but are unique to the challenge of finding the perfect place for retirement living.

Finding the Perfect Place for Retirement Living

1. How much living space do you need or want?
2. What kind of climate is best for your life style or health?
3. How much money do you have to spend on a retirement house without limiting your retirement cash flow or savings?
4. If you sell your house do you have enough equity to pay for a retirement house?
5. Are there adequate health services in the area?
6. Do you enjoy being with the people in the new neighborhood?
7. What recreation facilities are available?
8. Are shopping and other services such as beauty salons and barbershops close by?
9. Have you spent enough time there to know if you enjoy being there?
10. If it is in a planned unit development, a retirement-park, or condominium, can you afford the amenities fees and the taxes?
11. What do the amenities include and who sets the price? Is there an elected board of a homeowner's organization who decides the rules and fees or does an owner? Have you read the rules?
12. Can you live with the rules of the area?
13. If you have a pet, are there adequate facilities and rules that will allow your pet to live there?

14. What are the prices of utilities and are they included in the amenities? Some include cable TV and some do not.
15. Do swimming pool, hot tubs and clubhouse facilities increase the fees beyond your ability to pay or do you think they should be a factor in you decision?
16. How do your children feel about you moving to the area? Have they visited it or will their lives be directly affected by your move?
17. What is the resale value of the property you are considering?
18. Are there specific rules about how you advertise if you choose to sell?
19. Is the area limited to seniors over fifty-five?
20. Does the area cater to senior citizens or resent them?
21. Do you feel safe in the area?
22. If something happened to your spouse, could you live there by yourself and be happy?
23. Do you already have friends or relatives in the area?
24. Do you enjoy being in a social group or do you prefer to live in more seclusion? Does the area allow for both life styles?
25. Will the area require a more expensive lifestyle than you can afford or feel comfortable in?

26. Do you have talents or skills that will enhance the lives of others in the area? How do you feel about sharing your talents?
27. Are there adult education programs that offer classes in some area you would like to pursue. Some small colleges take advantage of the expertise of retired professionals. Who knows? You may start a new career.
28. Are you willing to get out of your comfort zone? (You can do it for a few months at a time to test your resiliency.)

There are lovely retirement locations all over the country. Developments there are designed specifically, with the retiree in mind. Most of them are in the Sunbelt from Florida to California. Some are in more arid country like Arizona, part of California or Southern Utah. Those who choose to make their permanent homes in these areas vacation in cooler climates in the heat of the summer, often using those large motor homes they once thought would be their permanent homes. It is possible to have the best of both worlds.

While you are considering whether to move or not, start deciding what to keep and what to throw away. Everyone I know has accumulated so many things that they no longer need or want. Closets bulge and long forgotten old treasures fill the backs of shelves and drawers. There are several ways to clear it out.

What to Keep and What to Throw Away

1. Give all the things you have been storing for children back to them. You have to physically give them to them or they will never come and pick them up. As you empty closets of everything from baby dolls to wedding dresses, old baseball mitts to college files and yearbooks it takes determination to return them to their rightful owners.

Have them over for dinner and while they are involved with the family, sneak the STUFF out and put it in their vans. If they want to throw it away they can and you don't have to be responsible for it anymore. Let me warn you. If you just ask them to take it with them they will probably find an excuse to leave in a hurry and forget it. After all, where are they going to put it? Or, the really mean way to get even with them for having stored it for so long, is to give it to their children. Then you can listen to the screams of, "Where did you get that? They are my old baseball cards. Oh, not my cheerleading megaphone. Don't you dare read my old diary!"

2. Pull all the rest out and have your married children claim anything they want before you throw it away. Or
3. Choose specific things you want a person to have and give it to them before the big give-away. Or
4. Put it all out for a garage sale. Have your children help you price the items and run the sale for you. (You will be surprised at how any things go home in their vans from the garage sale.)
5. Donate it to a goodwill store. Get a receipt and deduct it from your taxes.
6. If you want to take the time, make a list of everything and what you did with it. I wish I had because I keep looking for things I once had and can't remember if I sold it, kept it or gave it away.
7. All of the above.

Some clean out specialists will tell you to sort things in three piles. One for things I know I want to throw away. One for things I would like to keep and one for things I would like to think about for a while. Get rid of the throwaways immediately. Put the things you want to save in their proper place and leave the other pile in plain view until you are sick of it and force yourself to make a decision about its demise. (That could be the start of your garage sale inventory.)

We learned the hard way how necessary it is to clean out and clear out. We helped care for an elderly relative who lived out of state. Before she passed away we had encouraged her to move closer to us but she refused saying she didn't want to have to clean out her house. I reminded her that someone would have to do it one day. She smiled and said, "I know that," as she looked me straight in the eye. I just wish I had asked her about the value of some of the treasures we undoubtedly threw away. Those of us who were left to empty the house and make decisions as to what to do with sixty years of "treasures" did not enjoy the task. After that experience my husband and I were determined that we would do everything possible to avoid leaving our children in that position. There we go again, trying to make life easy for our children. Will we ever learn? Probably not. Read on.

It took us two years to give away and sell what we didn't need. After spending winters in a second house we had also accumulated several duplications of small appliances and other household items. When we finally made the move to our retirement home our grandsons were furnishing a condo to live in at college. It was the perfect situation to help them set up their kitchen and share some of the extra furniture we had. We enjoy going to see them and find them using some of the things we had enjoyed buying and using.

This is all a part of deciding where you want to live and how it will affect the enjoyment of your retirement. I am not suggesting that everyone should move to a retirement Mecca but I am suggesting that you weigh the options. Many retirees stand to live twenty to twenty-five years. That is long enough to enjoy more than one location. Enjoy deciding!!!

Chapter Seven
Re-create Yourself

Now is the time to look for new talents to surface, new interests to blossom or even old skills to be refined. The first few years after retirement could be compared to a crash course in retirement renewal.

Choosing something that exercises your body, something that exercises your mind and something that is restful and relaxing is a good balance. You don't have to do everything today or tomorrow but you will want to get involved in something soon.

One of my friends who had worked in the pressures of the medical field for many years found painting to be her challenge and fulfillment. It started with watching the demonstrations on television. She had always enjoyed crafts and as a part of that she had taken classes in tole painting. Moving to oil painting was a natural. After watching the TV demonstrations she sent for a video that she could put on freeze until she was ready for the next step. She purchased the minimum set of brushes, paints and a canvas. The joy she felt in watching her paintings materialize before her eyes, was more than she had ever expected. Now she has painted hundreds of pictures, taken classes, hung her pictures in a lovely restaurant and sold several. The important thing is that she doesn't have to do it to earn a living but just for the enjoyment and personal satisfaction. Part of that satisfaction is being able to share the fruits of your labor with others. Giving pictures to family and friends and observing their appreciation is all the pay she needs. However, she is now accepting money for special paintings she does by commission.

Another artist friend found returning to the art she loved in High School was just what she needed to fight depression. It did become a career for her and brought joy and beauty to many of us who have purchased her paintings.

So many of us have been caught up in the competition and judgement meted out by grades, etc. in work or school. Now we can put that all aside and just enjoy the experimentation with various types of media. Another friend enjoys the challenges of watercolors, while another prefers to work with acrylics. Several of my friends and I took some lessons from an accomplished painter who had trained with an artist who specialized in the wet on wet oils method. It was fun to shop for our supplies and take the class together. Some of our paintings were not too bad, with the help of our instructor. You can always clean off the canvas and start over. At least, that is what I did several times. This is not just an avenue for women. Men also enjoy painting.

My point is that you can experiment with different talents. It doesn't cost too much and if you approach it as recreation you can find a lot of fulfillment even if you have limited talents in that expertise. A by-product of this endeavor is that you become more aware of the world around you. If you don't find that you have the skill to put what you see on canvas, you can still look at the shadows, variation of colors and shapes in the beauty that surrounds us. It also opens the door to appreciation of the visual arts from modern artists as well as the old masters.

Physical exercise can enhance your retirement years like nothing else. Much has been written about the roll of fresh air and exercise to mental health also. My husband and I set out on a walking regimen. We started with a few blocks at a time and in just a few days had increased the distance to three miles a day. I lost weight, which was our primary goal, but the best reward was the time we spent together. We talked about a lot of things, from joys and disappointments with extended family to some of our personal concerns. We found we were closer together in our thinking and had learned to appreciate each other more. We also had a desire to eat more nourishing food and slept better. We let the excuse of being too busy or tired keep us from continuing this regimen.

After recalling the benefits we had from it I am determined to get back to it. At least as soon as the weather is a little better and I have rested.

Living in a retirement area affords many different kinds of exercise. Ours is one that is in a climate that allows year-round outdoor activities. Water aerobics is a popular one and some swim several laps a day. Some of us are still trying to get brave enough to appear in swimming attire before our friends. (Adding another mile a day may be a step toward the water regimen.) Another benefit of the pool has been for people with various kinds of health problems. Hip and knee replacements are common to the senior citizen population. Several who are wheelchair bound find swimming pools and hot tubs provide a therapy that enhances the healing and restoration to health. Again, another benefit is the social interaction that gets them away from a life of seclusion and helps them make new friends.

Dancing has really caught on with the retirement segment of our society. Line dancing is a real boon to single men or women who can have fun and exercise dancing without the necessity of having a partner. Square dancing groups provide opportunities for making new friends while you exercise. Callers charge a nominal fee and provide the music and instruction. Attending square dancing conventions and workshops affords opportunities to travel to new locations with friends.

Golfing is seen as one of the most popular activity for retirees. It certainly is in the top ten. It also gets you outside and though it doesn't provide the best aerobic exercise it is great recreation for those who enjoy the sport. Here again, there are all degrees of expertise among golfers but somehow they seem to group together with others close to their own expertise. In my case, I am invited to go with a group because I make them feel guilty if they don't invite me and I always make them feel better because I seem to end up with the highest score.

I was golfing with my son one day and told him I just had to buy a driver with a larger head. I was sure it would improve my score. He lovingly said, "Mom, what you need are lessons." I'm sure I do and one of these days when I get caught up with my writing I'm going to do that. The rest of the story is that the following Mother's Day the doorbell rang and there on my porch was a new set of clubs with graphite shafts. It was a gift from my son. I bought myself a new bag and visor but it only cut my score by two. At least I don't embarrass my friends with my old stuff. I am a good sport at golf parties too when I get the "goofy golfer" award.

One of the favorite golfing activities in our group is the weekly golf scramble. We draw to see which hole we start on and every foursome is made up of two women and two men. We play best ball so it is a way to move along and learn from other golfers. The course is a par three with some challenging sand traps and water. For those of us who are not serious golfers or who are not able to play a full course, it is an opportunity to enjoy the game and socialize with friends.

Another good exercise is bicycle riding. It is amazing how many older people enjoy bike riding for exercise. Like they say, "You never forget how, it is just like riding a bicycle." It didn't work for me but it sure works for a lot of people I know. I think it takes some kind of built in balance that wasn't included in my gene bank. I've already told you I fall down fishing. Why would riding a bicycle be any different?

Crafts groups are also popular with retirees. Some craft shops will provide instruction but another source is to have a member of the group teach each other the crafts they have learned over the years. A friend of ours does southwest art with sand held in place with zippers. His "zipper art" is unique and he graciously teaches others this art. Another friend designs greeting cards from a variety of materials and also teaches calligraphy. Quilts are made in our clubhouse and anyone who likes to quilt or learn to quilt is invited to help. Sometimes they are made for an individual but several are made for fund raisers to help pay for the activities that go on in the park. Crocheting patterns are often shared for an afghan and/or many other items.

Our retirement park has a craft shop with a wide variety of power tools and space to construct fairly good size projects. My husband enjoys woodworking and the craft shop was a big factor in our deciding to locate in this park. He has made several nice pieces of furniture and is now specializing in birdhouses which we enjoy decorating.

Reading is a favorite pastime and good books make the circuit as friends and neighbors share them with each other. A nice supply of paperbacks and jigsaw puzzles are available for exchange. It is not uncommon to see a particularly challenging puzzle started in the clubhouse. Warning! Do not stop by to find and place one piece. They are addictive.

Most retirement areas are close to good size bodies of water, so if your thing is sailing or other water sports, those are available also. There are also cool canyons not far from some of the retirement sports where you can enjoy a few days away without a long trip or just a picnic in the pines.

Communities in retirement areas publish lists of available activities. There are community or junior colleges in many of the areas in the retirement zones that offer classes in almost every discipline. The most popular are computer classes designed for any level of expertise in technology. They also provide opportunities for mentoring programs in different areas of expertise.

Small groups of people with similar interest seem to find each other. Genealogical research interests some while others like to share poetry they have written by reading it aloud to an appreciative group. This can open new avenues to thought also. After listening to a friend read some of her cowboy poetry I thought, "That sounds like fun and since I have some Western background I'll try some also." My thoughts took me back to the high Uintah Mountains in Utah where my husband and I had gone on a horseback overnight trip with some friends from a riding club. This is what I wrote:

Ridin' The Shale

Late afternoon, reinin' 'round ma horses head
Followin' the trail the outfitter led,
Sometimes windin' and sometimes straight.
Daylight was burnin', it'd soon be late.
The trail was steep and we passed the pine
To the shaley top 'bove the forest line.
The dew was settlin' o'er the terrain.
And a shiver shook my female frame.

Dusk was fallin' fast and the first star shone.

The wrangler called, "Hold on to yer saddle horn.
Walk em slow. Don't let em have their head.
This shale is slick and they ain't bin fed.
Soon as we neer the camp we've made
They'll try to jump the ditch and you'll be laid
On that hard old shale with a broken bone.
No EMTs er amb'lances ta take ya home."

I grasp the horn and held my breath
As sure as shootin' I was facin' death.
But the wise old horse knew better'n me
And he could see what I couldn't see.
He picked his way o're the slippery shale
Eased down in the ditch and up the swale.
They pried my hands from the saddle horn
And helped me off. My thoughts were torn.

There I wuz in this lofty terrain
And the only way down was the way I came.
A night in the bedroll may calm ma fears.
No one knew ma fright or saw ma tears.
Sure as night turned in ta day
I wuz on that horse the same old way.
'Cept for this time I'm goin' down
And I can't wait ta get in ta town.

Just ta let me know ma fears weren't fer naught
That horse uf mine balked and the more I fought

The more he reared and bucked me off.
I landed where the dirt wuz soft.
No bones wuz broke but ma pride wuz hurt.
I slapped his rear, and kicked the dirt.
I told him what fer in an angry voice.
But I rode him out. I had no choice.

(Needless to say, this was very confusing to the spell and grammar check on my computer.)

Creating a lifestyle full of recreation and intellectual challenges will enhance and possibly lengthen your life. It may even start you on a whole new career if you are not careful. *Or it may not.* When I ask my distributor about the possibilities of publishing a book of cowboy poetry he said, "Well, in the industry, they say poetry is the kiss of death." Since I am doing everything possible to avoid death, I decided to write this book instead.

Chapter Eight
Feeding Your Spirit

Deciding what to include in this chapter has brought me to the realization that people look on spirituality in different ways and it is not my intent to change your religious beliefs. My purpose in writing this chapter is to help you, as you read it, and me as I write it, to examine those things in our lives that enrich our existence and bring us joy. Joy is what this book is about. If we don't pursue things in our lives that stimulate our thoughts and raise us to a higher level of thinking and appreciation we will certainly be less than we could be.

One of the tragedies of life is seeing a friend or loved one become bitter and disheartened. Age sometimes brings with it challenges that try the spirit and sense of wellbeing. Grumpy old men might make good fodder for a funny movie but I think it demeans the older segment of our society. Hopefully, we can be funny without being GRUMPY. What may seem funny to a younger generation is just part of living for us. The other day as I was trying to step into a pair of slacks I laughed at myself, realizing I looked exactly like my impersonation of an old lady when I was in a high school drama class. I must remember to have that full length mirror in my bedroom replaced.

The loss of a spouse or a lingering illness can test our inner self and we either survive it with a better understanding of who and what we are or we despair of ever feeling joy again. An accepted theory of modern philosophers is that as people face their own mortality they are more likely to turn to the spiritual and artistic aspects of life. Unfortunately, too many of us wait for a serious illness or tragedy in our life to bring us to our knees in prayer.

Music is one of the mediums that touches the heart. It can make us laugh or cry or move us to a whole spectrum of feelings. The sounds and words of music elicit memories of long forgotten feelings. For us the "oldies" are most popular as they remind us of happy days or even sad days. Songs of World War II bring nostalgic memories of saying goodbye but also happy feelings of ultimate joy when loved ones survived and came home. The sounds of music that turn our hearts to days of courtship and school days are precious.

We are often moved to more spiritual feelings as we listen to religious refrains or we are stirred to patriotism by the lively marches heard at a parade. Sometimes our thoughts are turned to better times and sometimes to those that brought heartache. Heart seems to be the operative word. Our spirit is fed by those feelings that touch our heart.

Make music a part of your life as a listener or performer. You may have always wanted to play the piano but never took the time. You can learn a new skill like playing the piano if only for your own enjoyment. Perhaps you played an instrument in the school band and haven't touched it for years. Pull it out and play to your hearts content. You may be surprised at how fast the skill comes back to you. There may be others that would enjoy a jam session with you. Nothing helps you appreciate the music performed by others as trying to play it yourself.

Another musical skill is singing. A chorus of mature voices can do wonders with the right kind of director. We have a church group that produces great, maybe not perfect, but great choral numbers. Our director is so skilled and has a personality that makes singing fun. So what if we have to take more breath breaks than the score calls for. With enough numbers and a creative director we can cover for each other. At least they cover for me all the time. If I hold my mouth just right, no one knows that there is no sound coming out. That is probably when the chorus sounds its very best. We all look forward to the winter months when we can start singing together again.

Poetry is a medium that drives my inner spirit. It may have that affect on yours as well. The modern poets, humorous poets or the time worn masters of the past spark in me a desire to read between the lines, to discover the rest of the story that was pared down to fit the meter. So much of poetry reflects the best of the writer's thoughts.

A good book can be inspiring also, opening new avenues of thought. Living life's experiences vicariously with the characters of a novel or a biography can inspire us to survive our trials that may seem small in comparison. What can be better than a lively discussion of a thought-provoking book with a friend? I loan some of my favorites to friends, especially a book that has been helpful to me as I have dealt with hard problems.

Live productions of music or drama bring so much more to the soul than does the trivia so often filling the television and/or movie screens. Look for lectures on subjects of interest to you and invite friends to go along with you so you can discuss it later.

Look at the benefits of friendshiping neighbors. Time often weighs heavy on those that don't get out of the house very often. An invitation from a friend can lift the spirit and redirect the outlook on life. Shared recipes and tips on how to make good pie crust can cement new friendships. You also have to find someone who will listen to you tell about your grandchildren so they can share their family stories with you. There is nothing like having a new friend that you can pour your heart out to. It helps you put things into perspective and you usually find out that all families have some of the same problems. The men compare fishing tips, how to repair cars or their favorite golf club. They like someone to confide in also, other than their wife. I really think they confide with each other about the trials of living twenty-four hours a day with their wives as well.

Some groups like to get together to play cards, dominoes, board games or just crazy parlor games. One group insists that anyone who leaves for any length of time is to bring back a new game or a new way to play an old game. How many ways can you play dominoes? It finally got to the point that we play it a different way, depending on whose house we play in. We call it house rules. After a good game, lots of laughs and delicious dessert we can go home to a good night's rest.

When I walked into church last Sunday, I suddenly felt at home and at peace. As I looked around I could see the same peaceful look on the faces of the rest of the worshipers. One friend shared with me as we walked out, "I haven't been in a church for years. It made me feel so good again." He wiped a tear from his eye with a weathered hand and walked to his car. Sometimes we just have to give it a chance to touch our hearts.

Someone has said that we can never come to terms with the ups and downs of our lives until we can look at it with God's perspective. How can one read the Twenty-third Psalm without being stirred spiritually? We are missing an important aspect of our lives when we lack a spiritual dimension. Life sometimes leads us to get so caught up in careers or families that we let the most important things slip by us. Fortunately, we have some retirement years to lift our hearts to higher levels.

Staying in touch with old friends or relatives can also enrich your life. How fun it is to open a letter from an old friend that says something like, "I've been thinking about you and just had to write you a note. Let's stay in touch." The other day I pulled up my e-mail and found a note from my high school debate partner who lives on the other side of the country. One of my dear friends had one of the best formulas for feeding the spirit. He said every day he made two telephone calls to friends and wrote two notes of appreciation or congratulations. He was the sort that built your spirit every time you saw him by greeting you with a smile and a sincere concern for your welfare. Can I take a leaf from his book to lift another? I hope so.

Prayer is a lifeline to God's will. Man is that he might have joy and have it more abundantly. A joy that comes from the simple life without competition or the need to climb to the top is a joy we can feel in our retirement years. As I contemplated that concept I was reminded of an old friend and was moved to make another effort at Cowboy Poetry.

CHAPS

He hung the stained and scared old chaps
On the nail in the bunk house wall.
The cattle was all rounded up
Out on the winter range this fall.

The leaves had turned to gold and red
And the air was coolin' mighty fast.
It had been a long hot summer,
This and them that he'd seen pass.

He and his chaps had seen 'em all
Since he was just a lad.
Now his bones was achin' with the storm
And his chest was hurtin' bad.

He could've spent his life
Wearin' fancy, city wraps,
A workin' in his pa's law office
But he'd chose to wear his chaps.

He'd had no wife or kids
Ter complicate his life
But now he felt right sorry
He hadn't had that strife.

He didn't think he'd wear those chaps
Or round up no more cattle.
The Doc said his days was numbered
And he'd pert neer lost the battle.

He'd make it right with the man up stairs
An sure hoped he'd fergive his little sins.
He's the last of the old cowboys an he'd bin told

"The one in the last round up is the one that always wins."

The chaps still hang on the bunkhouse wall
Covered with dust, but we recall
The cowboy who once owned 'em.
The stains on the chaps tell a tale of him,

Who did his work from dawn to dusk,
A man who knew his real worth
Was an honest pay, a little grub
And a place to bunk on God's good earth.

Open your life to some spirituality and bring joy to your life!!!

Chapter Nine

You and Your Family

Children really do care about you and want your happiness and good health. Include them in your plans and help them understand your reasoning for your decisions. It is sometimes just as hard on them to have you leave the old stomping grounds and move on. They need an opportunity to understand that life goes on and you can't go home, because home doesn't stay the same as the home they remember. Most of us, including our children, need to learn how to say goodbye to the past and build on it for a happier future.

Our oldest son went back to visit the house we had raised our children in and sold twenty-five years ago after all of our children were married. It broke his heart to see it in such disrepair. The once manicured lawns were over grown, windows boarded up and a bank notice tacked to the door. My husband and I designed and built the house. We have many happy memories of the years spent there with our family but when it no longer met our needs we had to move on. Our son, very philosophically, wrote to his father, "Your handiwork is no longer manifested in wood, glass, Formica and linoleum... but it has been eternally transformed to the lives of your children and grandchildren who bear your name permanently for all to admire. Happy Father's Day."

Including family pictures and memorabilia in the decor of your retirement house help them feel that they have not lost touch with their roots. It also allows you to have your precious memories around you. We can't find joy without taking the best of our past with us.

Grandchildren enjoy an occasional trip to your retirement retreat. A swim in the pool and some time on the putting green can be a drawing card. What they like most however is watching the old videos of family Christmas parties and looking through the photo albums. One grandson loves to peruse the books on the shelves and find one he likes. Seeing him curled up in a corner reading one of our favorite books, looking so at home, thrills us. We hope he will always come to us.

We always get teased about rolling the sidewalks up at 8:00pm but our response is, "We have no sidewalks, just lawn and grass and quiet." In spite of our quiet life style we still convince them that it is cool to come to our house for Thanksgiving or other holidays. In fact, the grandchildren like to bring friends

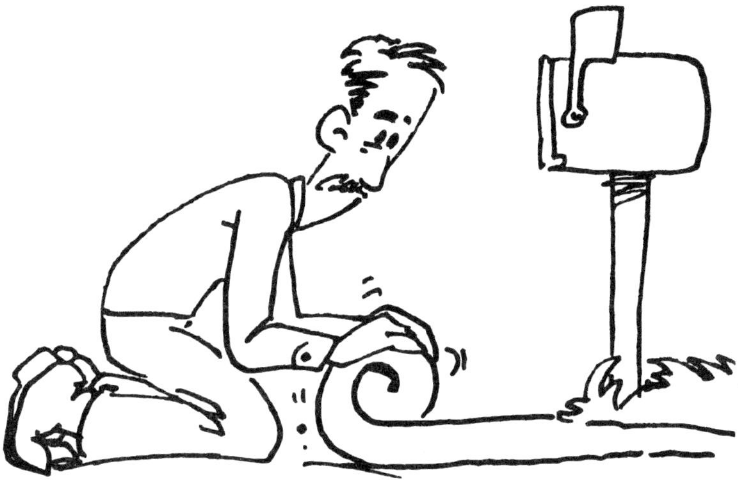

here to get away for a day or two. Sometimes they just sleep and eat here but they are always welcome and it is fun to meet their friends. We have already started traditions that involve family coming to our retirement home. The family golf scramble has become one to look forward to.

We go to our children's homes for special occasions when we are invited. Sometimes we can accept the invitation but there are times when distance and or weather prohibit it. Retirement carries with it the right to say, "Sorry, we can't make it this time."

Telephones and e-mail make communication easy and we stay in touch. I tell my friends that big telephone bills are still more economical than the big grocery bills I had for family Sunday dinners. I do miss cooking a big family meal so I invite friends over. Cooking for just the two of us is not as rewarding.

Let your children know where your important papers are and who to get in touch with if they can't find you in an emergency. Share with them what you have done with your family trust and who is responsible to make decisions if you are not able to make them for yourselves.

Our refrigerator still has the grandchildren's pictures displayed with magnets. You don't have to give up family just because you move to another location. Did you notice how easy it was for them to move all over the country to work or for some other need? You have the same right and you can all live with it.

The other day we were able to tend our first great grandchild while his parents attended a wedding in our area. It was so much fun and we were glad they chose us to care for him. Do we continue to be our granddaughters, grandparents? Does she still love us and turn to us when she needs us? Of course, and your grandchildren will also.

Children and grandchildren are proud of parents and grandparents who continue to take charge of their own lives as long as they are able to do so. In today's world, that should be a long time. Most of us have dreaded a time when we would be dependent on our children and choosing the right retirement life style can put that day off for years to come.

Now that we have decided that retirement is going to be fun and joyful, we will not become grumpy old grandpas and grandmas and our kids will love it.

We had just the right example of a grandma who knew how to live life in an upbeat way. She lived to be eighty-four, drove a car up to the end, dressed in bright colors, wore high heels, had her hair done every week and painted her own nails. Always having something to laugh about, our children loved to have her around and have memories of a happy grandmother. We can enjoy retirement if we put our heart into it and share the happy part of it with our children.

The cartoons in this book have been created by our grandson. I'm sure you will see that he sees us as comical and happy, which we are. It also shows that families can be close and work together without living side by side. I would far rather have my grandson make fun of me in cartoons and laugh with me than complain that I was an old, grouchy lady.

Our family consists of two daughters, two sons, two son-in-laws and two daughter-in-laws. We also have seventeen grandchildren, twelve grandsons and five granddaughters and one grandson-in-law. Now we have one great grandson. They all have to hang the Christmas stockings I have crocheted for them. (At least when we are at their house for Christmas.) Do they know they have a grandpa and grandma? You can be sure of that! I wouldn't let them forget and I can tell you what grade they are in, how old they are and the last time we talked.

You can stay close to family after you retire and make it a meaningful, positive relationship.

Chapter Ten

What Do You Do When You're Done?

You could go back to the beginning of the book and make a list of all those things you haven't done yet. I've written about a lot of options and if you have chosen some of them I'm sure there are others you missed. Maybe you just weren't interested and that is OK. I just hope that you have found some things to make you happy. You may even have had a chuckle or two.

During the ten years we have been retired my husband and I have both survived cancer, sold our big house, and built a retirement house. We have traveled, and enjoyed old and new friends as well as family. We have celebrated our 50th high school reunions where we renewed old friendships, and our 50th wedding anniversary. We have published two books and still have ideas for more. There is still so much left to do.

I have boxes of pictures that need to be put in

albums or thrown away. There are letters left to write and several books on my bookshelf I haven't read yet. There are so many places to travel. There were sixty-four listed in the travel catalogue and the golf magazine I read in the doctors office this morning had at least a dozen more. There is plenty to do. You are never done.

Write you're own history. I'll bet it is better than mine. I haven't written it yet. I started going through old pictures and couldn't decide which ones to keep and which ones to throw away. Why did I keep the ugly ones? I put the lid on the box and put it away until I can handle accepting the fact that I really did look like that when I was eleven. Review your life and write about it. What a wonderful legacy you can leave to your family and friends. If you can write and laugh about your past it will help your progeny face their lives with a smile or determination to improve on the past.

If you haven't kept a journal there are other things to help jog your memory. School yearbooks and pictures, letters you have received and tucked away, planners or yearly calendars, and visits with old friends are just a few to use as references. There is so much being written about the war years and the fifties now that has brought back memories of where we were and what we were doing. It is amazing how your grandchildren love to pick your brain about those times. I, for one, am afraid that my "part time" memory will allow me to let some of the best be lost to forgetfulness.

I have always been a news buff. I rely on the newspapers and television to keep me abreast of current events. With children and grandchildren in different parts of the world, we find it mandatory to subscribe to newspapers. One reason is for the news and the weather and the other is for the crossword puzzles. Oh, yes, we also have to check the obituaries from our hometown paper. I think that is a malady of aging but my excuse is that I want to remember the surviving members of the deceased's family. There is a lot of interesting information in obituaries that you would miss if you didn't take time to read them. Since this book is about enjoyment, I will just throw this admission in. I do smile on occasion when I find out the real age of someone who always kept it a secret. But that's it for my confessions for the day.

A crossword puzzle can take up to half the morning to solve. On the other hand it can be whipped off in a few minutes. I can not understand why they have to throw in all those movie directors, actors, authors and strange middle names of people. (Hint) If you slide it under the stack of magazines you can get the answers the following day. Would I do that? As I said, "I'm not confessing."

Consider another volunteer venture if you still have time on your hands. Pink ladies are always in demand at hospitals. When we seem to fill our calendars with more appointments for doctors than for friends it is wise to make friends with some health care professionals. Get acquainted with your local health care givers before you need their services.

Hey, you can even take a nap in the afternoon. I was enjoying that respite so much and then some specialist on TV had to inform me that you were to call them *power naps* and that they should only last from fifteen to twenty minutes or you wouldn't be able to sleep at night. That took all the fun out of it. Now they tell me it will make me feel more ambitious. When do we get to rest in this life without feeling guilty? I'm not sure I'm going to find more ambition but I will surely be *powerful*. If one works, two

should work twice as well. I can't sleep at night anyway. My next book may be, "What to Do In The Middle of the Night When You Can't Sleep" or "Insomnia Antics".

There is so much to look forward to. We are going to the next Branson Christmas shows. There are two or three good movies we haven't seen and I haven't read the sequel to the book I just finished. We have sixteen more grandchildren to get married and have kids. Four will be in college next year and two will graduate from high school. Three are on two-year missions for our church and one is ready to leave on a mission. Our son just called and said their family was moving to Japan. With all those things going on do you think we are going to sit around and feel sorry for ourselves? Not on your life! The advertisement for something we won't discuss here says, "We've got a lot of living to do" and we are going to enjoy it. Take time to count up all the things you have to live for and you will find a smile on your face and a reason to: *Kick Up Your Heels and Enjoy Retirement at Its Best.*

Prologue

If you think of other ways to enjoy retirement don't call me, just do it! I'm too busy to answer the phone and I am probably still laughing about that joke my friend told me. No I can't remember the joke, but I still feel like laughing.

My email address is jbthom@redrock.net. A positive comment on the email may encourage me to keep writing. Criticism will hurt my feelings but may improve my writing. I can always delete it.